Is It Treason?
Or Not?

The Constitution's Law of Treason and the American Perception in the 21st Century

Susan M. Wendler

abbott press

Abbott Press books may be ordered through booksellers or by contacting:

Abbott Press
1663 Liberty Drive
Bloomington, IN 47403
www.abbottpress.com
Phone: 1 (866) 697-5310

Because of the dynamic nature of the Internet, any web addresses or links contained in this book may have changed since publication and may no longer be valid. The views expressed in this work are solely those of the author and do not necessarily reflect the views of the publisher, and the publisher hereby disclaims any responsibility for them.

Any people depicted in stock imagery provided by Thinkstock are models, and such images are being used for illustrative purposes only.
Certain stock imagery © Thinkstock.

ISBN: 978-1-4582-1893-3 (sc)
ISBN: 978-1-4582-1891-9 (e)

Library of Congress Control Number: 2015904702

Print information available on the last page.

Abbott Press rev. date: 6/19/2015

For the men and women who selflessly serve our country and protect our rights and liberties, and for Uncle William, a WW II veteran. There never was a truer red, white and blue heart.

Preface

The question of what actually constitutes treason first became of interest to me after hearing public comments made during a foreign dignitary's visit to the U.S. At that time I realized that a large amount of the general public possibly does not have a clear idea of what actually constitutes treason under our nation's Constitution.

The purpose of this book is to enlighten the general public and therefore raise both the level of understanding of current events and the dialogue regarding them. It is in no way to be considered as possible legal advice or defense for any act.

My gratitude for assistance with this project and their kind patience goes to the librarians of the Tarlton Law Library at the University of Texas in Austin, Texas and the librarians at the Faulk Central Library in Austin.

My thanks also to Sekou Kante, Kevin Foran, and the team at Abbott Press for taking on this project, along with their encouragement and assistance.

Susan M. Wendler

Contents

Introduction

Volumes of material have been written about the history and various interpretations of the, what many call deceptively simple, two-sentence clause defining treason in Article III of the U.S. Constitution. Why do we need more? In a time when hostilities between political parties are becoming stronger and wars are becoming more complex, understanding this issue becomes even more important. The purpose of this book is to simplify and help clarify in the average citizen's mind what is actually treason under the law of our Constitution. With such clarification, a citizen should be able to form more knowledgeable opinions of current affairs and news events. My research certainly improved my own understanding and perspective and hopefully it will do the same for other people.

I started this journey by poring over old history books and law encyclopedias, wanting to form my own opinions and conclusions. Near the end of the road I discovered that at least two other authors, more eloquently articulate and learned on the subject than I am, had already written similar works. Specifically, law professor Carlton Larson wrote in 2006, a lengthy article for The University of Pennsylvania Law Review, titled "The Forgotten Constitutional Law of Treason and the Enemy Combatant Problem" and, in 2002, Mark Holzer, also a law professor, wrote "Why Not Call It Treason? From Korea to Afghanistan" for The Southern University Law Review. [1]

Since the historical facts surrounding the Constitution's Article III law of treason and court cases are what they are, Larson and I appear to have followed the same path of research. However, Larson delves deeper into each fact, focusing on the concepts of allegiance and enemies, reminding us that the Constitution's Article III Treason Clause prohibits the military from exercising authority over certain categories of individuals. The history of the concept of allegiance is an integral part of the concept of treason and those individuals who owe allegiance to a country, either as citizens or temporary residents, are the individuals subject to the charge of treason and have been traditionally tried in civilian (non-military) courts. As you read Article III Section 3 you will note that the clause specifies "in open Court" as opposed to military commissions or tribunals, along with specific restrictions set in its wording, and punishment set by Congress.

Professor Larson, through extensive legal research, and I, through basic research, proud American common sense, and awareness of traditions, arrive at similar simple conclusions. (See Part III and IV of this book for my conclusions.)

For the reader who would like to read deeper and has access to these law review journals, I highly recommend Professor Larson's work; although in my opinion, care should be taken not to take some statements out of context for better understanding. He also lists extensively more reference articles for further reading.[2]

Mark Holzer's article in <u>The Southern University Law Review</u> is worthwhile reading for a different perspective on the subject, with Holzer's focus on espionage and aid to the enemy.

Holzer, in this author's opinion, presents a very different argument as to the relevance of the term "levying war" to the prosecution of treason, separating "levying war" and "adhering to their enemies" in Article III's definition into two separate events, based on the use of the word "or" between them. (See Holzer's note at the end of his article.) [3]

Separating the two events into two non-related independent events, ("prongs"or branches of the clause, as Holzer and some writers refer to them) would allow prosecution of espionage (giving them aid) as treason regardless of war status. In other words, overt acts committed during times of peace would be prosecutable as treason. I personally do not believe this interpretation was the Framers' intention, as it would make the clause less restrictive and open up the possibility of abuse.

Holzer noticeably does not expound upon Supreme Court Chief Justice John Marshall's well-known landmark 1807 opinion in the Aaron Burr treason case, which does consider the existence of war, actual or constructive levying of war, as a crucial element for the prosecution of treason, with the use of force being the main criteria, with or without a formal declaration of war. (See Part II of this book for my summary of the main points of Chief Justice Marshall's opinion.)

Wherever appropriate, I have referred to what I interpret Larson's and Holzer's opinions to be, with proper credit to them.

Also, considered to be one of the leading authorities of the twentieth century on the constitutional law of treason, James Willard Hurst (1910-1997) collected his law review articles into the book <u>The Law of Treason in the United States</u> (1971).[4] I do not recommend this book to anyone other than serious students of constitutional law as it is rather "heady" reading and is, at times, a little confusing on certain points. Like the writers that I have already mentioned, Hurst examined the same works of early English writers that Chief Justice John Marshall analyzed. Being a more recent writer, though, than Marshall, Hurst does, however, make some interesting observations regarding the decline of the use of the doctrine of constructive treason (Hurst, Chapter 5), and is also enlightening about individual state's actions regarding treason (Hurst, Chapter 3). His main focus and contribution to the subject, though, (in my opinion) is his analysis of the restrictiveness of Article III, Section 3, and the intent of the Framers, as evidenced by their personal notes, the Committee of Detail's notes in the draft of the Constitution, and the Constitutional Convention's discussions (Hurst, Chapter 4). Hurst analyzes the possibilities of the Framer's intent at constructing a restrictive clause down to setting limits to the offense;

protecting domestic political debate and non-violent dissent, along with freedom of speech of individuals; protecting individual security by strengthening evidentiary protection against perjury; preventing the doctrine of constructive treason (which had been a problem of British legislative and judiciary history); limiting judges and legislators by defining where authority lay and by doing so, also preventing the military from having any jurisdiction over civilians; and probably most importantly, protecting against abuse by use of the charge against political foes (Hurst, Chapter 4).

Though, if one has read or reads the Federalist Papers, most of the Framers' intent at restrictiveness can already be gleaned from them.

Hurst also picks apart the concept of intent and the overt act as it applies on the accused's side. (Hurst, Chapters 5 and 6)

I can only hope that my own work makes the subject matter more accessible to the general public, and that the flowchart I devised for Part III helps simplify and organize thought on the circumstances of a situation, making informed opinions on an important subject easier. This book is intended only to help educate general public opinion and is in no way to be considered as possible legal advice or defense for any act.

PART I
Definition of Treason

U.S. history owns claim to one of the most notorious traitors in modern society. His name is forever linked with treason and his story is well known.

Benedict Arnold, a trusted friend of George Washington, became disgruntled at lack of credit for his brilliance, bravery, and successes in battle and decided to sell out his soldiers and command post, West Point, New York, during the Revolutionary War, to the British for British gold, along with other benefits.[5] (Sources differ as to the monetary amount.) His punishment? Although he escaped capture, Arnold died persona non grata in London, scorned even by the British.[6]

Today, in the 21st century, when one thinks of treason, what is the first situation that comes to mind? *Your* mind? An American-born young person fighting with the Taliban against American soldiers in a Middle Eastern country? An American-born terrorist plotting on American soil? A multinational company, that began as a small American grown company, siding with a foreign government on some issue? A protester burning the American flag? An American political figure or political body yielding some of the nation's sovereign authority to an international governing body?

That situation or action, when it occurs, may shock you down to your red, white, and blue blood and bones, but is it really treason, a hanging offense unless pardoned by the President himself? Or is it a lesser felony that should be prosecuted as such? Or is it prosecutable at all?

Origin of Definition in Founding Documents

The obvious place to pinpoint the original American definition of treason and the intent of this country's Founding Fathers is in our founding documents: the Declaration of Independence, the Articles of Confederation, the U.S. Constitution, and, while not a document, but considered by historians to be one of the most important political works in our nation's history, the Federalist Papers. The Federalist Papers, authored by the Framers of the Constitution, James Madison and Alexander Hamilton, along with John Jay, argued the inadequacies of the Articles of the Confederation and the need for the U.S. Constitution.

The word "treason" is not found in the Declaration of Independence. However, to preclude and to defend against the accusation of treason, committed by the colonists against the British king, the authors of the Declaration announced to King George III and the rest of the world in 1776, that the colonies considered themselves absolved of allegiance to the British crown:

> "That these United Colonies are, and of Right ought to be, FREE AND INDEPENDENT STATES; that they are absolved from all Allegiance to the British Crown, and that all political Connection between them and the State of Great-Britain, is and ought to be totally dissolved; and that as FREE AND INDEPENDENT STATES, they have full power to levy War, conclude Peace, contract Alliances, establish Commerce, and to

3

do all other Acts and Things which INDEPENDENT STATES may of right do."[7]

This concept of allegiance that the colonists absolved themselves of has played throughout history and still plays today a major role in determining whether treason has been committed.

Between the 1776 Declaration of Independence and the 1787 ratification of the U.S. Constitution, there were the Articles of Confederation, the short official title being the "Articles of Confederation and Perpetual Union".[8]

Drawn up in 1777 -78 by the delegates of the first 13 states, consisting of New Hampshire, Massachusetts, Rhode Island, Connecticut, New York, New Jersey, Pennsylvania, Delaware, Maryland (Maryland was the last state to sign in 1781.), Virginia, North Carolina, South Carolina, and Georgia, the Articles of Confederation were thirteen articles that as a whole formed a "friendship" pact between these states.

All discussion of the legislative and political actions of the individual states regarding treason aside (This can be found elsewhere, one source in particular being Hurst's Chapter 3), the Articles of Confederation, like the Declaration of Independence, also do not contain a definition of treason. The actual definition does not appear until written later into the 1787 U. S. Constitution Article III. However, the Confederation Articles do bring up the issue of states' rights and their jurisdiction over treason in the Confederation's Article IV, which states:

> "If any person guilty of, or charged with, treason, felony, or other high misdemeanor in any State, shall flee from justice, and be found in any of the United States, he shall, upon demand of the Governor or executive power of the State from which he fled, be delivered up and removed to the State having jurisdiction of his offense. Full faith and credit shall be given in each of these

States to the records, acts, and judicial proceedings of
the courts and magistrates of every other State."[9]

The only other mention of treason in the Articles of Confederation
is in Article V, referring to the exclusion of treason from the protective
privileges of members of Congress:

> "Freedom of speech and debate in Congress shall not
> be impeached or questioned in any court or place out
> of Congress, and the members of Congress shall be
> protected in their persons from arrests or imprisonments,
> during the time of their going to and from, and
> attendance on (sic) Congress, except for treason, felony,
> or breach of the peace." [10]

The inadequacies of the Articles of Confederation led to work on the
U.S. Constitution in 1787 by the Federalists, who were those in favor
of a stronger central government.

The Framers (or authors/architects) of the Constitution were
expressly authorized by the Confederation Congress to revise the
Articles of Confederation with "alterations and provisions therein" that
would render the new federal constitution "adequate to the exigencies
of government and the preservation of the Union." (See the Federalist
Papers essay Number 40.)[11] Thus, the wording in the above Articles
of Confederation regarding states' rights of jurisdiction over treason
and exclusion of treason from congressional privileges is also used in
the U.S. Constitution Article No. IV, Section 2 and Article No. I,
Section 6.

And, in keeping with the 1776 quest for freedom from tyranny,
the "Founding Fathers", and James Madison in particular, added a very
restrictive definition of treason into Article III, Section 3 of the new
U.S. Constitution:

"Treason against the United States, shall consist only in levying War against them, or in adhering to their Enemies, giving them Aid and Comfort. No Person shall be convicted of Treason unless on the Testimony of two Witnesses to the same overt Act, or on Confession in open Court.

The Congress shall have Power to declare the Punishment of Treason, but no Attainder of Treason shall work Corruption of Blood, or Forfeiture except during the Life of the Person attainted." [12]

The term "levying war" in the first sentence of the definition was borrowed from the 14th century British Statute of Treason under King Edward III and has been analyzed by a multitude of authoritative writers, both British and American. The writers most often referred to for assistance in interpretation are the 17th and 18th century writers Lord Edward Coke, Judge Matthew Hale, Judge Michael Foster, the highly esteemed Judge William Blackstone, William Hawkins, and Revolutionary War attorney James Wilson. The most exhaustive analysis of the term, though, and also the most well-known, might be U.S. Supreme Court Chief Justice John Marshall's circuit court opinion in the 1807 Aaron Burr trial, discussed in Part II of this book.[13]

Simply put, to levy war against the U.S. is to attempt to overthrow or overturn the U.S. government by use of force. And as Chief Justice Marshall succinctly states at one point in his court opinion "There is no difficulty in affirming that there must be a war or the crime of levying it cannot exist,…".[14]

Prosecutors sometimes use the doctrine of constructive levying war, where the design is not to overturn the government but to accomplish another purpose by the use of force, such as preventing a tax law from being executed. The purpose of the use of the doctrine of constructive levying war is to bring an action into the realm of treason, and prosecutable as such. This practice has engendered a great deal of criticism from many historians and legal authorities. (See Part II for further discussion.)

According to <u>Gale Encyclopedia of American Law</u>, hereafter referred to as GEAL, the term "Aid and comfort", in the first sentence of the definition, (during times of war) would refer to any act that betrays allegiance to the U.S and has the effect of weakening the ability of the U.S. to attack or defend itself against its enemies. This would include such acts as furnishing the enemy with supplies, classified information, transportation, and shelter. But according to GEAL, the intent must be there, rather than accidently or unintentionally, in order to be convictable as treason under the Constitution.[15]

Thus, the importance of the word "overt" in the second sentence of Article III Section 3's definition. An overt act would be an open or public act that is meant to accomplish a treasonous intention.[16] It must be more than an act of preparation, and to be convictable as treason, must be witnessed by at least two people. The requirement for at least two witnesses is extremely important. Not one witness, not hearsay evidence, not assumptions, not conjectures. Only the testimony of at least two witnesses to the same overt act is acceptable for conviction of treason charges.[17]

The intent and the act are equally important. Simply put, a treasonous intent without an overt act is not treason, and a treasonous act without intent is not treason. Such questions may arise as, at what point must intent be shown and how it is to be evidenced. Then the judge and jury must decide the answers, keeping in mind the authority of set precedents (rulings and decisions made by previous judges and juries in similar cases).

Although Article III does not actually state the words "during times of war", GEAL interprets the Article III treason clause as applying only to acts committed during war, or war being levied. Peacetime disloyal acts are not considered treasonous under the Constitution.[18] The reference book does not cite a basis for this conclusion but it appears to be drawn from the traditional interpretation of the two phrases "levying war" and "adhering to their Enemies" as being dependent on each other. However, peacetime disloyal acts may be prosecuted as some other lesser crime.

There has been much written that tries to separate "levying war" and "adhering to their Enemies" into two separate independent instances of treason, as mentioned in the Introduction. However, traditionally, adhering to enemies or aiding enemies with information in peace time is prosecuted as espionage, if it meets the criteria for espionage, or some lesser felony.

Since Congress, on its own, does not have the power to change the Article III Section 3 definition of treason, those crimes that would appear to be treasonous, but are not by definition, have been made by Congress into lesser felony crimes. Some of these are misprision of treason (concealment of treason) and seditious conspiracy, and are set down in the collection of legislation known as U.S. Code, as explained further in Part II of this book.

The second paragraph of Article III Section 3 does give Congress the power to set the punishment, and in 1790 and 1862 the punishment was set as death as the maximum punishment and the minimum penalty being 5 years imprisonment and $10,000 fine. (See U.S. Code Title 18 Section 2381). The second paragraph of Article III Section 3 also forbids the punishment of treason being extended to family ("blood") or inheritances (no "Forfeiture except during the Life of the Person attainted.")

In all, treason is mentioned four times in the U.S. Constitution, being specifically:

- Article I, Section 6 on Congressmen's Privileges from Arrest
- Article II, Section 4 on Presidential Removal from Office for Treason

- Article III, Section 3 on the Definition
- Article IV, Section 2 on States' Rights Regarding Jurisdiction

A fifth section, Article II, Section 2, does not specifically mention, but implies treason, in the Presidential Powers of Pardon:

> "and he shall have Power to grant Reprieves and Pardons for Offenses against the United States, except in Cases of Impeachment."

Alexander Hamilton, in the Federalist Papers essay No.74, argues the case for not including the word "treason", for the purpose of prevention or deterrence. Knowing that they could be pardoned might embolden traitors, according to Hamilton. (See his quote from essay No. 74 below.)

Proponents' Arguments in the Federalist Papers

Before the new Constitution was ratified in 1787, a series of essays, 85 in all, appeared in New York City newspapers under the title "The Federalist". Written by the principal architects of the U.S. Constitution, James Madison and Alexander Hamilton, along with John Jay, under the pen name of Publius, these essays were intended to raise the tone and increase the enlightened reasoning in the national debate on the ratification of the Constitution. They were in particular aimed at the voters of the New York state ratification convention.

Known as the Federalist Papers, the essays addressed the deficiencies of the Articles of Confederation mainly in essays No.1- 40, and the need for the new Constitution.

The issue of treason is brought up in Federalist Papers essays Nos. 43, 74, and 84.[19]

In essay No. 43, James Madison argues for the inclusion in Article III, Section 3 of Congress's powers of punishment, along with the restraints placed upon those powers:

> "As treason may be committed against the United States, the authority of the United States ought to be enabled to punish it. But as new-fangled and artificial treasons have been the great engines by which violent factions, the natural offspring of free government, have usually wreaked their alternate malignity on each other, the convention have, with great judgment, opposed a barrier

to this peculiar danger, by inserting a constitutional definition of the crime, fixing the proof necessary for conviction of it, and restraining the Congress, even in punishing it, from extending the consequences of guilt beyond the person of its author."[20]

In Federalist Papers essay No. 74, Alexander Hamilton argues for presidential powers of pardoning, as written in the Constitution's Article II, Section 2, Paragraph 1:

"and he shall have Power to grant Reprieves and Pardons for Offenses against the United States, except in Cases of Impeachment."

In arguing the case of whether to bestow the powers of pardoning treason in the legislative branch or the President, Hamilton concludes:

"But the principal argument for reposing the power of pardoning in this case in the Chief Magistrate (Hamilton referring to the President) is this: in seasons of insurrection or rebellion, there are often critical moments when a well-timed offer of pardon to the insurgents or rebels may restore the tranquillity (sic) of the commonwealth; and which, if suffered to pass unimproved, it may never be possible afterwards to recall. The dilatory process of convening the legislature, or one of its branches, for the purpose of obtaining its sanction to the measure, would frequently be the occasion of letting slip the golden opportunity. The loss of a week, a day, an hour, may sometimes be fatal. If it should be observed that a discretionary power with a view to such contingencies might be occasionally

conferred upon the President, it may be answered in the
first place that it is questionable, whether, in a limited
Constitution, that power could be delegated by law; and
in the second place, that it would generally be impolitic
beforehand to take any step which might hold out the
prospect of impunity. A proceeding of this kind, out of
the usual course, would be likely to be construed into an
argument of timidity or of weakness, and would have a
tendency to embolden guilt."[21]

In other words, the ability of the President to act quickly to
pardon treason, as opposed to possible procrastination or delays by
the legislature, could act to calm the nation. But actually writing this
specific ability to pardon treason into the Constitution might have, in
Hamilton's opinion, the effect of encouraging rebels to think they could
act with no consequences.

And finally, Federalist Papers essay No. 84, addresses whether or
not the inclusion of a Bill of Rights within the text of the Constitution
was necessary. The author of this particular essay, Hamilton, points out
specific provisions that in themselves, in his opinion, constitute a Bill
of Rights, one of them being the restrictions on the definition of and
punishment of treason.[22]

The Bill of Rights did not become a part of the text of the Constitution
in 1787; they were added separately in 1791 as amendments, further
protecting against tyrannical charges of treason by the enumeration of
free speech and free press rights, along with other rights of the people.

British Heritage

While the U.S. Constitution has as part of its roots Great Britain's vast and complicated history of the treatment of treason (enough for another whole book and not within the scope of this book), this history appears to serve more as a basis for backlash than as building blocks, except for the laws under King Edward III in the 1300's.

Many historians credit the 14th century British Statute of Treason (1351) under King Edward III as being the foundation block of the U.S. Constitution's Article III treason clause. It seems strange, doesn't it, that the Framers of the Constitution, even though they were well educated, being in a new country and possessing deep convictions and desire for freedom from persecution, would need to refer back 400 years for the simple two-sentence restrictive wording of the definition in Article III. The protection of freedom, under these circumstances, won hard through war with Great Britain, would seem instinctive. Apparently, they felt the time-tested wording of the British Statute of Treason was necessary to lend credibility and strength to Article III.

Carlton Larson in his UPLR article points to the Revolutionary War attorney James Wilson as being most responsible for the use of the British Statute language in our Constitution's treason clause.[23] Wilson apparently was a great admirer of the statute's legal strength. Hurst, in Hurst's Chapter 4, also suggests Wilson's heavy involvement as a member of the Constitutional Convention's Committee of Detail.

They, the architects of the Constitution, and many authoritative writers and judges have relied on this 14th century British law, and its associated interpretations, for guidance because of its restrictive nature, the same restrictiveness incorporated into our Constitution.

In all, our nation's Constitution, with this restrictiveness, makes it clear that the accusation of treason is not to be used to control the populace or political foes.

PART II

Legislative Actions and Historic Judicial Actions

Although Congress was not given the power by the Constitution to expand or change the definition of treason found in Article III, what it could and can do, is make acts that seem treasonous, but do not fall under the strict constitutional definition of treason, felonies and punishable under U.S. Code Title 18.[24] These do not carry the death penalty. Use of force or violence is the chief characteristic determining the eligibility and the magnitude, or feloniousness, of the crime.

The Legislature's U.S. Code Title 18

Both the acts and punishment can be found in U.S. Code Title 18, Part I, Chapter 115, Sections 2381 – 2390, with Section 2381 restating the constitutional definition of treason, along with its punishment, and Sections 2382 thru 2390 the lesser felonies. Published every six years by the Office of the Law Revision Counsel of the U.S. House of Representatives, the U.S. Code is the classification by subject matter of the general and permanent laws of the United States, and can be accessed on the internet at U.S. Code.house.gov. or uscode.house.gov.

Sections 2381 thru 2390 consist of:

Sec. 2381. TREASON

"Whoever, owing allegiance to the United States, levies war against them or adheres to their enemies, giving them aid and comfort within the United States or elsewhere, is guilty of treason and shall suffer death, or shall be imprisoned not less than five years and fined under this title but not less than $10,000; and shall be incapable of holding any office under the United States."

Sec. 2382. MISPRISION OF TREASON

"Whoever, owing allegiance to the United States and having knowledge of the commission of any treason against them, conceals and does not, as soon as may be, disclose and make known the same to the President or to some judge of the United States, or to the governor or to some judge or justice of a particular State, is guilty of misprision of treason and shall be fined under this title or imprisoned not more than seven years, or both."

Sec. 2383. REBELLION OR INSURRECTION

"Whoever incites, sets on foot, assists, or engages in any rebellion or insurrection against the authority of the United States or the laws thereof, or gives aid or comfort thereto, shall be fined under this title or imprisoned not more than ten years, or both; and shall be incapable of holding any office under the United States." (AUTHOR'S NOTE: Notice this and the following section cover what might have been treated earlier as constructive treason.)

Sec. 2384. SEDITIOUS CONSPIRACY

"If two or more persons in any State or Territory, or in any place subject to the jurisdiction of the United States, conspire to overthrow, put down, or to destroy by force the Government of the United States, or to levy war against them, or to oppose by force the authority thereof, or by force to prevent, hinder, or delay the execution of any law of the United States, or by force to seize, take, or possess any property of the United States contrary to the authority thereof, they shall each be fined under this title or imprisoned not more than twenty years, or both."

Sec.2385. ADVOCATING OVERTHROW OF GOVERNMENT

"Whoever knowingly or willfully advocates, abets, advises, or teaches the duty, necessity, desirability, or propriety of overthrowing or destroying the government of the United States or the government of any State, Territory, District or Possession thereof, or the government of any political subdivision therein, by force or violence, or by the assassination of any officer of any such government; or

Whoever, with intent to cause the overthrow or destruction of any such government, prints, publishes, edits, issues, circulates, sells, distributes, or publicly displays any written or printed matter advocating, advising, or teaching the duty, necessity, desirability, or propriety of overthrowing or destroying any government in the United States by force or violence, or attempts to do so; or

Whoever organizes or helps or attempts to organize any society, group, or assembly of persons who teach, advocate, or encourage the overthrow or destruction of any such government by force or violence; or becomes or is a member of, or affiliates with, any such society, group, or assembly of persons, knowing the purposes thereof--

Shall be fined under this title or imprisoned not more than twenty years, or both, and shall be ineligible for employment by the United States or any department or agency thereof, for the five years next following his conviction.

If two or more persons conspire to commit any offense named in this section, each shall be fined under

21

this title or imprisoned not more than twenty years, or both, and shall be ineligible for employment by the United States or any department or agency thereof, for the five years next following his conviction.

As used in this section, the terms "organizes" and "organize", with respect to any society, group, or assembly of persons, include the recruiting of new members, the forming of new units, and the regrouping or expansion of existing clubs, classes, and other units of such society, group, or assembly of persons."

Sec. 2386. REGISTRATION OF CERTAIN ORGANIZATIONS

(AUTHOR'S NOTE: This lengthy section lists the types of organizations and organizational activities that require registration with the U.S. Attorney General. To avoid tediousness for the reader I have quoted only part of Sections (B) (1) and (D).)

"(B)(1) The following organizations shall be required to register with the Attorney General:

Every organization subject to foreign control which engages in political activity;

Every organization which engages both in civilian military activity and in political activity;

Every organization subject to foreign control which engages in civilian military activity; and

Every organization, the purpose or aim of which, or one of the purposes or aims of which, is the establishment, control, conduct, seizure, or overthrow of a government or subdivision thereof by the use of force, violence, military measures, or threats of any one or more of the foregoing.

(D) Whoever violates any of the provisions of this section shall be fined under this title or imprisoned not more than five years, or both.

Whoever in a statement filed pursuant to this section willfully makes any false statement or willfully omits to state any fact which is required to be stated, or which is necessary to make the statements made not misleading, shall be fined under this title or imprisoned not more than five years, or both."

Sec. 2387. ACTIVITIES AFFECTING ARMED FORCES GENERALLY

"(a) Whoever, with intent to interfere with, impair, or influence the loyalty, morale, or discipline of the military or naval forces of the United States:

(1) advises, counsels, urges, or in any manner causes or attempts to cause insubordination, disloyalty, mutiny, or refusal of duty by any member of the military or naval forces of the United States; or

(2) distributes or attempts to distribute any written or printed matter which advises, counsels, or urges insubordination, disloyalty, mutiny, or refusal of duty by any member of the military or naval forces of the United States—

Shall be fined under this title or imprisoned not more than ten years, or both, and shall be ineligible for employment by the United States or any department or agency thereof, for the five years next following his conviction.

(b) For the purposes of this section, the term "military or naval forces of The United States" includes the Army of the United States, the Navy, Air Force,

Marine Corps, Coast Guard, Navy Reserve, Marine Corps Reserve, and Coast Guard Reserve of the United States; and, when any merchant vessel is commissioned in the Navy or is in the service of the Army or the Navy, includes the master, officers, and crew of such vessel."

Sec. 2388. ACTIVITIES AFFECTING ARMED FORCES DURING WAR

"(a) Whoever, when the United States is at war, willfully makes or conveys false reports or false statements with intent to interfere with the operation or success of the military or naval forces of the United States or to promote the success of its enemies; or

Whoever, when the United States is at war, willfully causes or attempts to cause insubordination, disloyalty, mutiny, or refusal of duty, in the military or naval forces of the United States, or willfully obstructs the recruiting or enlistment service of the United States, to the injury of the service or the United States, or attempts to do so—

Shall be fined under this title or imprisoned not more than twenty years, or both.

(b) If two or more persons conspire to violate subsection (a) of this section and one or more such persons do any act to effect the object of the conspiracy, each of the parties to such conspiracy shall be punished as provided in said subsection (a),

(c) Whoever harbors or conceals any person who he knows, or has reasonable grounds to believe or suspect, has committed, or is about to commit, an offense under this section, shall be fined under this title or imprisoned not more than ten years, or both.

(d) This section shall apply within the admiralty and maritime jurisdiction of the United States, and on the high seas, as well as within the United States."

Sec. 2389. RECRUITING FOR SERVICE AGAINST UNITED STATES

"Whoever recruits soldiers or sailors within the United States, or in any place subject to the jurisdiction thereof, to engage in armed hostility against the same; or

Whoever opens within the United States, or in any place subject to the jurisdiction thereof, a recruiting station for the enlistment of such soldiers or sailors to serve in any manner in armed hostility against the United States—

Shall be fined under this title or imprisoned not more than five years, or both."

Sec. 2390. ENLISTMENT TO SERVE AGAINST UNITED STATES

"Whoever enlists or is engaged within the United States or in any place subject to the jurisdiction thereof, with intent to serve in armed hostility against the United States, shall be fined under this title or imprisoned not more than three years, or both."

Espionage Act – Relation to Treason

Although espionage is usually "aiding the enemy", legislation deals with it separately from treason. While U.S. Code 18 Chapter 115 deals with treason and its associated felonies, espionage is dealt with under U.S. Code 18 Chapter 37 Sections 792-799. (Section 791 was repealed.) However, like treason, espionage does carry the death penalty if committed during war-time. Unlike treason, it does not carry the strict two-witness requirement for conviction.

Sections 792-799[25] consist of:

- SECTION 792 – Harboring or Concealing persons (AUTHOR'S NOTE: persons guilty of or about to commit Section 793 or 794)
- SECTION 793 – Gathering, Transmitting or Losing Defense Information
- SECTION 794 - Gathering or Delivering Defense Information to Aid Foreign Government
- SECTION 795 – Photographing and Sketching Defense Installations
- SECTION 796 – Use of Aircraft for Photographing Defense Installations
- SECTION 797 – Publication and Sale of Photographs of Defense Installations

- SECTION 798 – Disclosure of Classified Information (AUTHOR'S NOTE: classified information regarding cryptographic systems or communication intelligence.)
- SECTION 798A – Temporary Extension of Section 794.
- SECTION 799 – Violation of Regulations of National Aeronautics and Space Administration

The titles of the sections are fairly self-explanatory, and the full description can be found easily on the internet under U.S.Code. house.gov.

Sadly, in the last half of the twentieth century and the beginning of the twenty-first century federal prosecutors have had numerous opportunities to press indictments for espionage activity. Like Great Britain's history and treatment of treason, the U.S. history and treatment of espionage is enough material for another whole book and not within the scope of this book, particularly since the determination of espionage is expanding to include "information-gathering" or "stockpiling" sensitive and classified information and communicating with the media. Harold Edgar and Beeno Schmidt's 1973 Columbia Law Review article "The Espionage Statutes and Publication of Defense Information" criticizes the vagueness and possible unconstitutionality of the espionage laws and is a must-read for anyone interested in the subject. The 157 page article seeks and offers solutions to the problems created by the clash between national security and freedom of speech and freedom of the press (media), along with the "extraordinary confusion about the legal standards governing publication of defense information".[26]

Flag Burning or Desecration of U.S. Flag

Burning the U.S. flag seems like the ultimate act of raw treason, doesn't it? But by now you have probably realized that it does not fall under the constitutional definition.

Congress did legislate against this act in October of 1989. The statute, forbidding the desecration of the U.S. flag, was passed in response to the court case of Texas v. Johnson. There was not enough support for an actual amendment to the Bill of Rights. The U.S. Supreme Court has not upheld the statute, considering it an infringement on First Amendment rights.[27]

Historic Judicial Cases – Pre-WW II

Because of the difficulty of proving acts of treason, there has not been a large number of treason cases brought before the courts. The more historic judicial cases that have laid down groundwork, as precedents, are listed below in chronological order. Some were handled constitutionally correct. Some were questionably so, but still have prevailed through the years. At least one, John Fries's second trial, was considered as evidence in the impeachment proceedings (however unsuccessful) against the judge, Supreme Court Justice Samuel Chase.[28] (According to GEAL, early Supreme Court Justices served double duty during their Supreme Court periods, serving also in an assigned circuit court as a trial judge. Therefore, the early treason trials had both a Supreme Court justice and a second district judge sitting on the trial.) [29]

1795 – United States v. Vigol
United States v. Mitchell

As well known for treason as Benedict Arnold is, he was not captured and brought before the courts. Even if he had been captured, the Constitution had not been ratified yet and therefore it would not have been a federal case. That makes the trials of "Whiskey Rebels" Philip Vigol and John Mitchell in 1795 the first for treason under the newly adopted Constitution, according to historians of Historic U.S. Court Cases and GEAL.[30]

When Pennsylvania farmers against the whiskey tax of 1791, of which Vigol and Mitchell were a part of, became violent towards federal authorities, they became candidates for charges of treason, by levying war against the United States. This is one of the first uses by U.S. prosecutors of the doctrines of constructive levying war and constructive treason.[31] Both Vigol and Mitchell, convicted and sentenced to be hanged, were pardoned by President Washington, as were the rest of the participants.

Besides being the first real test of federal authority, the significance of this case lies in the precedent set by the "constructive" interpretation of "levying war against the United States", an interpretation made by the prosecuting attorneys and the judge. Justice Paterson instructed the jury that armed opposition to the enforcement of a federal law amounted to levying war, and therefore, treason.[32]

Historian and author of "Treason and the Whiskey Insurrection" for Historic U.S Court Cases, Mary K. Bonsteel Tachau argued that the prosecution's interpretation of levying war and the court decisions based upon it should have been overruled. Her criticism was based on the opinion that the defendants had not been engaged in war against the U.S. under the common understanding of the words.[33]

This precedent-setting loose interpretation of "levying war" in the Whiskey Rebellion case appears to "fly against" the constitutional Framers' intention to set a strict definition of treason.

1799 – 1800 United States v. Fries

In 1798, Pennsylvania was again the scene of another tax rebellion, this time a property tax rebellion, known as Fries Rebellion. The leaders, including a former captain in the Continental Army, John Fries, were arrested and charged with treason.

The precedent set in the Whiskey Rebellion trial prevailed in Fries's trial. The judge in the trial, District Judge Richard Peters, instructed the jury that preventing by use of force the execution of a federal law was treason. (Again, the use by prosecutors of the doctrine of "constructive levying of war".) Fries was convicted but granted a second trial after disclosure of juror prejudice, according to GEAL.[34]

Supreme Court Justice Samuel Chase, and again, District Judge Peters, presided over the second trial and distributed a pretrial summary opinion which outraged Fries's attorneys enough to withdraw from the case. With no representation, Fries was again convicted and sentenced to hang, but was later pardoned by President Adams. Adam's pardon in this case was apparently an official criticism of the use of "constructive levying war" (according to Hurst, pg.198).

1807 – United States v. Burr

The trial of Aaron Burr in the Richmond, Virginia federal circuit court in 1807, is considered the landmark trial for the definition of treason, or more accurately, for the interpretation of the U.S. Constitution's definition of treason. Unlike the proceedings of the four previous trials of Vigol, Mitchell and Fries (Remember, Fries had two trials.), the judge in Burr's trial, Supreme Court Chief Justice John Marshall, required a strict adherence to the Constitutional limits and the intent of the Framers of the Constitution.

As Vice President under Thomas Jefferson, 1801 to 1805, Aaron Burr was considered controversial by many and a rascal by some in Washington D.C.'s political and social circles. During his vice-presidency, he was indicted for murder for killing Alexander Hamilton, one of the Framers of the U.S. Constitution, in a duel that Hamilton had tried to avoid. Burr was neither tried nor convicted.

After his term as Vice-President was over, Burr supposedly organized a military expedition whose purpose was believed to be either an attack on Mexico and its possessions or separation of the western states of the United States into separate rule. Either goal was considered by President Jefferson to be treason by his political foe Burr.

Burr was arrested, tried, and acquitted. The prosecution was not able to provide two witnesses to the same overt (open or public) act of levying war, as constitutionally required and as per Chief Justice Marshall's instructions to the jury.

And, unlike the loose interpretation of levying war in previous cases, Chief Justice Marshall made clear his opinion that conspiracy to make war or intention to go to war does not constitute levying war. There must be actual war action with employment of force. A secret assembly, such as Burr's and his partner, General James Wilkinson, without further open action (actual employment of force) and without Burr being present at the time, did not constitute actual treason on Burr's part. (See discussion points below.)

The entirety of Chief Justice Marshall's lengthy landmark circuit court opinion, along with an 1807 letter to an associate, William Cushing, can be read in <u>John Marshall Writings,</u> edited by Charles Hobson.[35]

While known as a strong constitutionalist and Federalist, Chief Justice Marshall does not appear to have had a strong pre-trial opinion on the interpretation of the Article III clause. According to William Cranch's 1809 "Reports of Cases Argued and Adjudged in the Supreme Court of the United States in the years 1807 and 1808", Chief Justice Marshall was one of the four justices present when the opinions were given in the earlier related trial of Bollman and Swartwout, and Chief Justice Marshall delivered the summary opinion.[36] Yet, he later unpretentiously asked associates for advice on interpretations, as evidenced by his letter to Cushing a month before the Burr trial began and two months before his written opinion on the Burr trial.[37] Also, in his Burr opinion, as you will see in my points below, he appears, in addition to clarifying, to re-evaluate and analyze the Supreme Court decision and opinion in the Bollman trial in a way that makes it appear as though he was not involved.

Also, surprisingly, Marshall did not recuse himself from the trial, even though the defendant Burr killed Justice Marshall's friend, Alexander Hamilton, in a duel. Having understood the importance of the trial, Chief Justice Marshall apparently wanted to ensure that a correct precedent was set, enabling the concordance of future decisions among judges. He wrote his associate Cushing that if the case could be easily carried into the Supreme Court he would not be asking for opinions. But, according to Marshall, since district court judges must decide the cases for themselves, avoidance of contradictory decisions among the judges was important to maintain the credibility of the judicial system.[38]

His subsequent analysis in his circuit court opinion breaks down into the following main discussion points:

- Whether a man can be convicted of treason if he was not present, either legally or actually, when the war was levied. Marshall's conclusion: he can not.[39] ---What acts by a person would cause that person to be considered as part of the levying war. Marshall concluded that "those only who perform a part, and who are leagued in the conspiracy are declared to be traitors. To complete the definition both circumstances must concur. They must "perform a part," which will furnish the overt act, and they must be "leagued in the conspiracy." The person who comes within this description, in the opinion of the court levies war."[40] ---Marshall's analysis of past authoritative British sources on the question of what makes a person an accessory or principal in treason, and whether the British doctrine that all are principals in treason holds true in the U.S. Marshall concluded that the doctrine does not apply to the U.S., "the Constitution having declared that treason shall consist only in levying war".[41]

- Whether the overt act given as evidence of levying war in Burr's case actually amounted to levying war.---What constitutes levying of war.---What constitutes an assemblage of men that would amount to levying war.---Whether actual force must be employed to constitute levying war. Marshall's conclusion: Yes, force being used was required to constitute levying war .[42]--- Marshall also comments on another writer's work on the term "levying war" by adding his own comment "without which no act can amount to treason,..."[43] (NOTE: Remember the issue touched on in the Introduction of this book of the two "prongs" of the definition of treason? Marshall appears to be saying that the second "prong", adhering to their enemies, cannot amount to treason unless war is being levied.)--- Marshall's analysis of the opinion of the Supreme Court in the Swartwout and Bollman case, requiring an assemblage of men with treasonable purpose to constitute levying war and whether force was considered a necessary component. By omission, because it was not necessary for the Swartwout and Bollman case to be carried that far, the court did not declare that force was a necessary element for levying war. Marshall did not feel it was the intent of that court's decision to say that force was not a necessary element.[44] (Remember, Marshall was one of the four justices that sat on the Supreme Court Bollman case and delivered the summary opinion, as discussed above.)---Marshall's further analysis of the writings of various authoritative British sources regarding levying war, as he, correctly, believed the Framers of our Constitution drew from British sources for the understanding of terms regarding treason.---Marshall's discussion of the doctrines of constructive treason and constructive levying war where the object is not to overturn the government but to accomplish some other purpose through the use of force, such as prevention of tax collection.[45]

- Discussion of the specifics of an indictment for treason requiring that an overt act of levying war be specified in the indictment, along with the place the overt act occurred, and that the specific overt act be proved.---Whether or not the doctrine of constructive presence can apply to Burr's case as the prosecution contended. The overt act of levying war on Blannerhassett's Island being laid as the treason in the indictment, the constructive presence of Burr must be proved. Marshall's conclusion: Whether Burr was actually present (which he was not) or whether procurement is substituted for presence as being part of the overt act, either must by proved by two witnesses, as constitutionally required, and must have been committed within the district.[46] Conjectures, references, or reasoning are not acceptable proof. The difficulty of proving procurement does not justify conviction without proof. [47]

- Discussion of whether the accused is an accessory or principal, and if established that he is an accessory, (as advisor or procurer), whether or not he can be tried before the guilt of the principal in treason is established in their own separate prosecution.---Marshall's discussion and procedural ruling on the inadmissibility and irrelevance of all other testimony in the accused's case since the requirement for two witnesses to the same overt act (in this case, procurement or advisement in the place of actual presence at the assemblage of men) had not been met and the guilt of the principals (those present at the assemblage or the overt act of levying war as laid out in the indictment) had not been established.[48]

- Chief Justice Marshall's final instructions to the jury: "The Court have (sic) given its opinion: it has said, that yet, if the Jury can satisfy themselves of the guilt of the prisoner, by the evidence of two witnesses, they have the right to find a verdict of guilty."[49]

According to historians, the jury deliberated 25 minutes and then acquitted Burr.

In my experience, when reading Supreme Court Justice Marshall's lengthy and complicated opinion, care has to be taken not to attribute to Marshall as his own opinion, his discussion and conclusions of other courts' opinions.

1859 – United States v. John Brown

John Brown was a strong abolitionist involved in the Underground Railroad, a network of anti-slavery people helping slaves escape to the North. During the 1850's, Brown and his sons, along with other anti-slavery men, led violent raids on pro-slavery settlers in Kansas, Missouri, and Virginia, freeing slaves to escape.

His last stand was at the town of Harper's Ferry, Virginia where he and his men took control of the federal armory to obtain arms for slaves' use. Captured by U.S. Marines, Brown was charged with murder, conspiracy and treason against the state of Virginia.

Brown's trial is considered by many historians to be a sham with a predetermined outcome. Despite the delayed arrival of Brown's attorney and Brown's medical condition, the trial proceeded and Brown was convicted of all three charges and hanged, catapulting him into martyrdom for the cause of freedom and abolition.

The significance of the trial in terms of procedural errors in the prosecution of treason? Where do we begin? A charge of treason committed against the state of Virginia for a raid on a federal arsenal; tried in a state court rather than a federal court; lack of legal counsel in beginning proceedings; lack of constitutional restrictions on treason charges; boiling down to a picture of what Northerners considered Southern anarchy (according to The Oxford Companion to American Law)[50] and a type of prosecution for treason that the Framers of the Constitution had tried to avoid.

Note aside, Article IV Section 4 of the Constitution guarantees every state a Republican form of government and, upon application by the state to the federal government, protection from domestic violence. So while states traditionally prefer to handle their own affairs, treason against a state (a violent attempt to overthrow the state government) is usually turned over to the federal government to handle.

1868 – Proclamation of Pardon and Amnesty

President Andrew Johnson brought all Civil War prosecutions for treason to an end by issuing a proclamation of pardon and amnesty which pardoned both soldiers and the President of the Confederacy, Jefferson Davis.

Special Inclusions under the Treason Law

According to GEAL, special inclusions under the treason law include non-U.S. citizens who owe temporary allegiance to the U.S. and betray it, although GEAL does not cite any court decisions or legislation as a basis for this statement.[51] U.S. Code Title 18 Chapter 115 Section 2381 includes allegiance as part of the treason law by stating "Whoever, owing allegiance to the United States,…". How a non-U.S. citizen could owe allegiance, temporary or otherwise, to the U.S. is expounded upon by Larson in his UPLR article discussed in this Introduction.[52] Simply put, except for those persons who are part of an invading military force, any person who is present within the borders of the United States, either temporarily or otherwise, and is therefore receiving the benefit of the protection of the United States, owes allegiance to the U.S. during that time, and is therefore, subject to the law of treason.

Also included under the treason law are U.S. citizens on foreign soil aiding the enemy during war time. Mildred Gillars, known as Axis Sally during WW II, broadcasted propaganda for the Nazis and was convicted of treason. Iva D'Aquino, known as Tokyo Rose, broadcasted for the Japanese during WW II and was convicted, but due to extenuating circumstances, was pardoned by the President.

WW II Cases

In addition to the cases of Axis Sally and Tokyo Rose, a number of other treason and espionage cases came forth as a result of WW II, the most famous (and controversial) one probably being the espionage case of Julius and Ethel Rosenberg. The espionage acts of the Rosenbergs, giving information to the Soviet Union, were committed during war time and therefore drew the death penalty. Convicted under the Espionage Act of 1917, the Rosenbergs were executed. They had not been charged with treason because, even though it was war time, the United States and Russia were allies, not enemies, during WW II.[53]

One of the more significant treason cases to come out of WW II was Kawakita v. United States. Kawakita was of dual nationality, born in the United States of Japanese nationals. As a student in Japan he renewed his passport with an oath of allegiance to the United States. He stayed in Japan when WW II broke out and took a job as an interpreter in a Japanese factory producing war materials. Outside of his duties as interpreter, he abused American prisoners working in the factory to increase production. He was charged with treason based not on working for the enemy, since everyone needs to work, but on his conduct against the American prisoners that showed intent to aid the enemy in their fight against the United States. According to <u>Gale Encyclopedia of Everyday Law</u>, even though he was convicted of treason, his U.S. citizenship was revoked and Kawakita was deported back to Japan.

Doctrine of Constructive Treason

Article III, Section 3 of the Constitution is a very simple, (deceptively simple according to many) stringent concept that becomes complicated when prosecutors attempt to introduce the concepts of constructive treason, constructive presence, or constructive levying war, trying to expand or loosely interpret the constitutional definition.

In her strong criticism of the legal proceedings in the Whiskey Rebellion trial of Mitchell, described earlier in this chapter and published in <u>Historic U.S. Court Cases</u>, historian Tachau appears to view "constructive" as being creative, "broadly construing" meanings and overstepping the Framers' intent.[54]

Chief Justice Marshall in his pre-trial June 29th letter to his friend William Cushing, expresses doubts as to how far the doctrine of constructive treason should be carried in the United States. In his later circuit court opinion in Burr's trial, Marshall defined constructive treason and constructive levying war and other constructive terms as a situation where the direct design is not to overturn the government but to accomplish some purpose by force,[55] but Marshall does not go so far as to explicitly state that he considers these doctrines as not legitimately falling under the constitutional definition. He does maintain that if these doctrines are used, each case must be examined individually as to the appropriateness of the use.[56] Then the constitutional requirement for two witnesses and the constitutional requirements as to legal procedures must all be met.[57]

Fortunately, recent history has found this doctrine under such criticism and disfavor that it has not been attempted as much. More and more judges have required proof of specific intent to overthrow the government, rather than rioting over the execution of a particular law. However, knowledge of the doctrine is still necessary. Under these circumstances, a strong unbiased judge with knowledge of past abuses and reverence for the Framers' intent, becomes even more important. In addition to punishing those who have committed treasonous acts that are provable within the requirements of the Constitution, the rights of the citizenry must also be upheld under the rule of law.

PART III
Wendler Flowchart for Determining Charges of Treason

How is your original understanding of treason holding up now? You should now realize that many actions you or I might have been quick to label treasonous before, actually do not fall under the Constitutional definition of treason but are actually lesser felonies.

Based mainly on information from U.S. Code Title 18, Supreme Court Justice John Marshall's court opinion in the Burr case, the Gale Encyclopedia of American Law, and of course, the U.S. Constitution, the following flowchart was meant as a general aid to help form intelligent opinions on news events.

However, when cases reach prosecution, judge, and jury, each case must be considered individually while maintaining the rule of law and constitutional procedures and requirements.

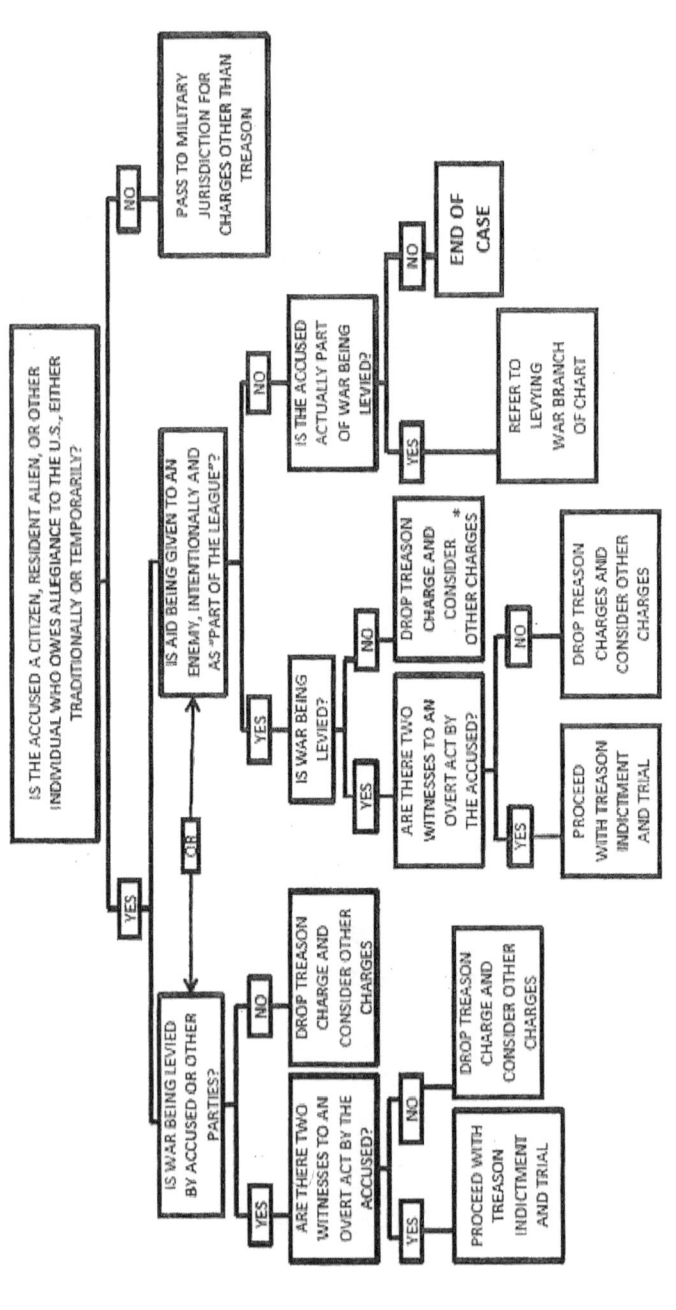

Wendler Flowchart for
Determining Charge of TREASON

Copyright © 2015 by Susan M. Wendler

* THIS IS THE POINT WHERE THE "TWO PRONG" ARGUMENT TRIES TO SEPARATE FROM THE TRADITIONAL INTERPRETATION

BASED ON INFORMATION FROM THE U.S. CONSTITUTION, U.S. CODE TITLE 18, GALE ENCYLOPEDIA OF AMERICAN LAW AND SUPREME COURT CHIEF JUSTICE JOHN MARSHALL'S SUMMARY OPINION IN THE BURR TREASON TRIAL

PART IV
Post 9/11 Cases & Conclusions

The twenty-first century opened with war with al-Qaeda.

With the events of 9/11/2001 and the "war on terror", new complexities have been introduced. Public emotions run high over the issues of:

- Lack of prosecution for treason of American-born citizens committing treasonous acts.
- The pros and cons of the Patriot Act enacted for the "war on terror".
- Military versus civil trial for accused.
- Constitutional protection for non-American enemies.
- Designations of lawful or unlawful combatant versus enemy combatant. The term "enemy combatant" is considered by some to be an illegitimate term used by the Administration to maneuver around due process of law.[58]
- The designation of and treatment of American citizens as enemy combatants with lack of due process.
- Whether non-American terrorist "sleeper cells" living and training in the U.S. owe allegiance to the U.S. and fall under the Treason Law.

- What methods of interrogation are acceptable or unacceptable in the public's mind.
- How the rest of the world views our interrogation methods and whether or not, under the circumstances, we care how they are viewed.

The definitive must-read for both sides of thought on some of the above current issues could be considered to be <u>The Enemy Combatant Papers: American Justice, the Courts and the War on Terror</u> presented by Cambridge University Press.[59]

Before the events of 9/11/2001, an American citizen fighting with or aiding a terrorist group against the United States would have been charged with treason, among other things, and would have received due process of law under our constitution. With the 9/11 events, charges and convictions for treason have taken a back seat to the federal government's need for information to prevent further attacks. Of 10 well known terrorist cases, Americans Jose Padilla, Yaser Hamdi, legal resident Ali al Marri, American Taliban John Walker Lindh, and the American Lackawana Six, none were, to this writer's knowledge, convicted of treason, only lesser crimes (where convictions have actually been attained).

While I have not seen any significant public survey of American's opinions on these issues, I suspect that the majority of Americans feel as this writer does:

1. All accused, detained American citizens and legal non-American residents along with those non-citizens who owe temporary allegiance to the U.S., are subject to charges of treason and should receive immediate due process and constitutional protection and tried in federal courts. The charge of treason should not be taken off the table in exchange for information. The consequences of failure to convict of treason have been well

analyzed by Henry M. Holzer in his SULR article. It must still be used as a deterrent.

2. Non-American enemies (they do not fall under the above categories) are obviously not subject to treason charges, but also are not entitled to our constitutional protections including civil court proceedings. Military court is appropriate.

Reasonable means, humane but still effective, should be used to obtain information from non-American enemies to prevent further attacks. I believe that those of us who remember seeing videos of our people, both civilian and military, being mutilated by terrorists do not have a problem with simple humiliating actions to the terrorists, under official supervision, (even though the "degrader" is sometimes degraded in the process, in some people's opinion), if, and only if, it means protecting and saving innocent American lives, and our military personnel. However, "degradation" has been made illegal in the Uniform Code of Military Justice. (See U.S. Code Title 10, Chapter 47.)

It is the opinion of this writer that, as long as the accused, detained American citizen receives immediate due process of law and the rule of law is followed, then the analytical process followed by Chief Justice John Marshall two hundred years ago to determine whether treason has been committed, is still relevant. It still works---in a civilian federal court. (Although a strong case can be made, that with today's technology, an assemblage of men is not required. An individual can accomplish as much as an assemblage of men.)

But in a military commission, hearsay evidence is sometimes allowed. In Brigadier General Mark Martin's speech at the Institute of World Politics April 26, 2012, broadcast live on C-Span, the Chief Prosecutor for Military Commissions admitted that because of the difficulty of investigating war crimes, there was more allowance for use of hearsay evidence in a military commission than in a civilian court.

This would be unconstitutional for conviction of an American citizen accused of treason, because of the strict constitutional requirement for two witnesses of the same overt act for conviction.

As long as the Constitution of the United States continues to stand up to the current and future assaults on its validity and relevance, the people of the United States can continue to put their faith in a rule of law that was established by decent freedom-loving men who put tremendous thought and effort into its content. One only has to read the Federalist Papers to see and understand this effort, even though one may not agree on the role of the federal government as espoused by the Federalist authors.

Treason against a great country such as ours is despicable, but the charge must be considered carefully to avoid the injustices and abuses of the past, and the citizenry must understand its rights, along with understanding what actually constitutes the capital offense of treason under our Constitution.

Bibliography

Anderson, William, <u>The National Government of the United States</u> (New York: Henry Holt & Company, 1946-47).

Articles of Confederation.

Chambers, Henry E., <u>A Higher History of the United States</u> (New York: American Book Company and University Publishing Company, 1898).

Cranch, William, "Reports of Cases Argued and Adjudged in the Supreme Court of the United States, in the Years 1807 and 1808.", (New York: I. Riley, 1809).

Declaration of Independence.

Edgar, Harold and Beeno C. Schmidt, Jr., "The Espionage Statutes and the Publication of Defense Information", Columbia Law Review, May 1973.

<u>Encyclopaedia Britannica</u>, 14th Ed. (New York, 1938).

Finkelman, Paul, "Flag Burning and the Constitution", <u>Historic U.S. Court Cases</u>, 2nd Ed., (New York: Routledge, 2001) Vol. II.

<u>Gale Encyclopedia of American Law</u>, 3rd Ed. (Gale Cengage Learning, 2011) Vol. 10.

<u>Gale Encyclopedia of Everyday Law</u>, 3rd Ed. (Gale Cengage Learning, 2013) Vol. Two.

Greenberg, Karen J., Joshua L. Dratel, and Jeffrey S. Grossman, editors, <u>The Enemy Combatant Papers: American Justice, the Courts, and the War on Terror</u> (New York: Cambridge University Press, 2008).

Hall, Kermit L., Editor-in-Chief, The Oxford Companion to American Law, (Oxford University Press, 2002).

Holzer, Henry Mark, "Why Not Call It Treason? From Korea to Afghanistan", Southern University Law Review, 2002, Vol. 29.

Honigsberg, Peter Jan, Our Nation Unhinged (Berkeley and Los Angeles: University of California Press, 2009).

Hurst, James Willard, The Law of Treason in the United States (Connecticut: Greenwood Publishing Corporation, 1971).

Larson, Carlton F.W., "The Forgotten Constitutional Law of Treason and the Enemy Combatant Problem", University of Pennsylvania Law Review, April 2006, Vol. 154.

Madison, James, Alexander Hamilton, and John Jay, edited by Isaac Kramnick, The Federalist Papers, (New York: Penguin, 1987).

Marshall, John, John Marshall Writings, edited by Charles F. Hobson (New York: Literary Classics of the United States, Inc., 2010).

Morison, Samuel Eliot, The Oxford History of the American People (New York: Oxford University Press, 1965).

Tachau, Mary K. Bonsteel, "Treason and the Whiskey Insurrection", Historic U.S. Court Cases, (New York: Routledge, 2001) Vol. I.

U.S. Code.house.gov.

U.S. Constitution.

Endnotes

1   Larson, Carlton F.W., "The Forgotten Constitutional Law of Treason and the Enemy Combatant Problem", University of Pennsylvania Law Review, April 2006, Vol. 154, pgs. 863-926.

    Holzer, Henry Mark, "Why Not Call It Treason? From Korea to Afghanistan", Southern University Law Review, 2002, Vol. 29, pgs. 181-223. Retrieved at Tarlton Law Library at University of Texas, Austin, from HeinOnline May 21, 2012.

2   Larson and his associates have managed to find and consult an impressive array of sources of both current thought on current issues and centuries-old authoritative British and American thought, such as the original writings of Coke, Hale, Foster, Blackstone, and Wilson. See his footnotes for more information. The older sources are the same authorities used by Chief Justice John Marshall.

3   Holzer, pgs. 222-223.

4   Hurst, James Willard, The Law of Treason in the United States (Connecticut: Greenwood Publishing Corporation, 1971).

5   Morison, Samuel Eliot, The Oxford History of the American People, (New York: Oxford University Press, 1965), pgs. 249, 259, 261.

6   Chambers, Henry E., A Higher History of the United States, (New York: American Book Company and University Publishing Company, 1898), pg. 238.

7   Declaration of Independence, 1776.

8   Title according to William Anderson, The National Government of the United States, (New York: Henry Holt & Company, 1946-47), pg. 17.

9   Articles of Confederation, Article IV.

10 Articles of Confederation, Article V. (sic) is a term used in my work to indicate that what you are reading is not a mistake, but as it is in the original work.

11 Madison, James, Alexander Hamilton, and John Jay, edited by Isaac Kramnick, <u>The Federalist Papers</u>, (New York: Penguin, 1987), No. 40 (XL), pg. 260.

12 U.S. Constitution, Article III, Section 3.

13 Chief Justice Marshall's complete court opinion can be found in <u>John Marshall Writings</u> by John Marshall, edited by Charles F. Hobson (New York: Literary Classics of the United States, Inc., 2010), pgs. 286-338.

14 Marshall, pg. 287.

15 <u>Gale Encyclopedia of American Law</u>, 3rd Edition (Gale Cengage Learning, 2011).

16 GEAL, Vol. 7, pg. 381.

17 GEAL, Vol. 10, pg. 94.

18 GEAL, Vol. 10, pg. 93.

19 See Note 11 above for publishing info. Essay No. 43 (XLIII), pg. 279, Essay No. 74 (LXXIV), pg. 422, and Essay No. 84 (LXXXIV), pg. 473.

20 See Note 19 above, quote from Essay No. 43, pg. 280.

21 See Note 19 above, quote from Essay No. 74, pgs. 423-24.

22 See Note 19 above, Essay No. 84, pg. 473-477.

23 See Note 1 above. Larson, pg. 872.

24 <u>Encyclopaedia Britannica</u> (sic), 14th Edition (New York, 1938), pgs. 439-440.

25 Retrieved from U.S.Code.house.gov.

26 Edgar, Harold and Beeno C. Schmidt, Jr., "The Espionage Statutes and the Publication of Defense Information", Columbia Law Review, May 1973, pgs. 930 – 1087. The quote "extraordinary confusion" is from page 1087.

27 Finkelman, Paul, "Flag Burning and the Constitution", <u>Historic U.S. Court Cases</u>, 2nd Ed., (New York: Routledge, 2001), Vol. II, pgs. 887-890.

28 GEAL, 3rd. Ed., Vol. 5, pg. 8.

29 GEAL, 3rd. Ed., Vol. 2, pg. 184, Inset U.S. V. Aaron Burr.

30 Tachau, Mary K. Bonsteel, "Treason and the Whiskey Insurrection", <u>Historic U.S. Court Cases</u>, (New York: Routledge, 2001), Vol. I, pg. 34. GEAL, Vol. 10, pg. 379.

31 Tachau, <u>Historic U.S. Court Cases</u>, Vol. I, pg. 36. GEAL, Vol. 10, pg. 381.

32 GEAL, Vol. 10, pg. 381.

33 Tachau, <u>Historic U.S. Court Cases</u>, Vol. I, pg. 34, 36.

34 GEAL, Vol. 5, pg. 7.

35 See Note 13.

36 Cranch, William, "Reports of Cases Argued and Adjudged in the Supreme Court of the United States, in the Years 1807 and 1808", (New York: I. Riley,

1809), Vol. IV, pg. 93, retrieved from HeinOnline by Tarlton Law Library at the University of Texas, Austin.

37 Marshall's letter to Cushing, <u>John Marshall Writings</u>, pgs. 282-285.

38 Marshall's letter to Cushing, <u>John Marshall Writings</u>, pgs. 284-285.

39 Marshall's court opinion, <u>John Marshall Writings</u>, pg. 286.

40 Marshall's court opinion, <u>John Marshall Writings</u>, pg. 292.

41 Marshall's court opinion, <u>John Marshall Writings</u>, pgs. 290-291.

42 Marshall's court opinion, <u>John Marshall Writings</u>, pg. 295.

43 Marshall's court opinion, <u>John Marshall Writings</u>, pg. 288.

44 Marshall's court opinion, <u>John Marshall Writings</u>, pgs. 302-304.

45 Marshall's court opinion, <u>John Marshall Writings</u>, pgs. 294-298.

46 Marshall's court opinion, <u>John Marshall Writings</u>, pgs. 322, 327.

47 Marshall's court opinion, <u>John Marshall Writings</u>, pg. 328.

48 Marshall's court opinion, <u>John Marshall Writings</u>, pgs. 335-338.

49 Marshall's court opinion, <u>John Marshall Writings</u>, pg. 338.

50 Hall, Kermit L., Editor-in-Chief, <u>The Oxford Companion to American Law</u>, (Oxford University Press, 2002), pg. 72.

51 GEAL, Vol. 10, pg. 94.

52 See Note 1 above. Larson, pgs. 867-68, 874, 883, 891-894.

53 GEAL, Vol. 10, pg. 93.

54 Tachau, <u>Historic U.S. Court Cases</u>, Vol. I, pgs. 34-36.

55 Marshall's court opinion, <u>John Marshall Writings</u>, pgs. 294-295.

56 Marshall's court opinion, <u>John Marshall Writings</u>, pg. 314.

57 Marshall's court opinion, <u>John Marshall Writings</u>, pg. 331.

58 The origins, legality, and implications of the use of the term "enemy combatant" in lieu of "lawful" or "unlawful combatant" is covered by Peter Honigsberg in his book, <u>Our Nation Unhinged</u> (University of California Press: Berkeley and Los Angeles, 2009).

59 <u>The Enemy Combatant Papers: American Justice, the Courts, and the War on Terror</u>, edited by Karen J. Greenberg, Joshua L. Dratel, and Jeffrey S. Grossman (New York: Cambridge University Press, 2008).